# SHOW & TELL

# SHOW & TELL

WRITTEN BY
GIANCARLO T. ROMA

PHOTOGRAPHS BY
THOMAS ROMA

pH

POWERHOUSE BOOKS · NEW YORK

SHOW & TELL

For Mary

Published in the United States by powerHouse Books, a division of powerHouse Cultural Entertainment, Inc.
180 Varick Street, Suite 1302, New York, NY 10014-4606
telephone: 212 604 9074  fax: 212 366 5247  e-mail: show&tell@powerHouseBooks.com
website: www.powerHouseBooks.com

Front cover design by Giancarlo T. Roma
Typography by Marvin Hoshino
Duotone scans by Gist, New Haven · Printed and bound in Italy by SIZ, Verona

Library of Congress Cataloging-in-Publication Data:
Roma, Giancarlo T., 1991–
    Show & tell / written by Giancarlo T. Roma ; photographs by Thomas Roma.
        p.   cm.
    Summary: A collaboration between father and son, featuring the father's photographs with commentary by his son.
ISBN 1-57687-133-9
    1. Photography, Artistic — Juvenile literature. 2. Roma, Thomas — Criticism and interpretation — Juvenile
literature. 3. Brooklyn (New York, N.Y.) — Pictorial works — Juvenile literature. 4. New York (N.Y.) — Pictorial works
— Juvenile literature. [1. Photography, Artistic. 2. Brooklyn, (New York, N.Y.) — Pictorial works. 3. Children's
writings.] I. Roma, Thomas, ill. II. Title.

TR655 .R643 2002
770′.1—dc21                                                                                           2001058798
Hardcover ISBN 1-57687-133-9

A complete catalog of powerHouse Books and Limited Editions is available
upon request; please call, write, or find us on our website.

2 4 6 8 10 9 7 5 3 1
First edition · 2002

Two years ago, when I was eight years old, my dad asked me if I wanted to work on a project with him. He had an idea that I could write about some of his pictures for a book. I said I would try, but I wasn't really sure how the project would turn out or even how we would begin.

We started by talking about the kind of things that you can see in a photograph and how a picture can mean something to you. Things like shadows showing the time of day and leafless trees telling the time of year. That if you look hard enough you can discover things that add to the meaning of a picture.

Then my dad gave me a stack of pictures that I could select from. I looked through them all and chose one. I wasn't sure what to write, so I tried to think of a starting sentence to give the reader an open door to what I felt the picture was about. And from that point on, that's what I did. I'd usually start with an observation, then I would look at the picture and write my thoughts. When I'm writing, it's like digging. I start at the top and end way deep down.

My dad would keep changing the stack so I would have a bigger selection. I might choose a picture because I was in a certain phase, or because of the state of mind I was in. When I saw a picture that I wanted to write about, I would feel excited. Usually it was because I could relate to something in the picture — either something specific like baseball, or maybe because there was something that reminded me of something I care about.

Looking at art gives me a hungry, choked-up feeling. I get it because I'm looking at other people's lives and it's a mystery. I try to think of what might be going on in their lives and try to understand them from my own experiences.

I began writing this book in January 2000 and wrote the final piece in December 2000. Looking back, I think my dad wanted me to see the world through his eyes from my perspective and write about it. And that's what I did. While writing this book, I have experienced many different feelings: love, loss, happiness, loneliness, caring, and wanting. And I learned about how my dad saw unusual, usual, meaningful, ordinary things.

I feel as if my dad created a world for me by taking pictures. And while I was writing about a picture, I was living in that world. I hope you can come too.

Giancarlo T. Roma

# SHOW & TELL

# A SHARED MOMENT

This baby looks like he is really connected to his father. It is a special moment that they have together because dads usually have to go to work a lot. There is one thing that only dads can give—a scratchy face. The baby is teething on his daddy's chin and is feeling his dad's mustache with his nose. I still like the feeling of rubbing against my dad's face before he shaves. The pool in the background gives you a sense of gentle peacefulness. I like the way the houses peek out just over the fences, as if they're watching over them.

Both the dad and the son must be enjoying this moment. I think that because both their eyes are closed. They look so dreamy in this picture that it must be a very loving moment. The baby looks tiny in his dad's strong hands. I'm sure it makes the baby feel safe and comforted. They have a connection that can never be broken.

## A HANDMADE TREASURE

I count seven things with wheels in this picture. The kids who live here must want to be in action—to ride, to move, to go. I like to ride my bike or go down a hill on a sled, because when I'm going really fast I don't think about anything else. The homemade go-kart must have been made by kids. They used baby carriage wheels, wood, and a rope to steer with. I think it's beautiful, not in the way you'd think of a girl, but in an old-fashioned handmade way. If I made it with my friends, I would really treasure it.

## PRE-GAME JITTERS

The boy standing on the sidewalk is wrapping his arms around himself for some reason. It could be that he's cold, but it's probably because he's nervous about facing the pitcher since he looks like he's on deck. In fact, I just came back from baseball camp, and I know what it feels like to be afraid of failure. Baseball means a lot to me, and I sometimes feel nervous about not doing as well as I think I should.

In this picture the ball is about to be pitched. The batter is in his stance—all his attention is on the pitcher. When kids play street games like baseball or stickball, the pitcher faces the direction of the traffic so he can call time-out if a car happens to come. In Brooklyn, the street is their stadium.

If I don't get on base or if I make an error, I'm a little disappointed with myself. But when I do get a hit or make a good play, I feel a feeling that only athletes can understand. It's a feeling of relief, happiness, and accomplishment.

13

# HIGH NOON CAR

The car in this picture looks like it has been through some tough times, or even an accident or two. It's summer, but no one is outside because it's lunchtime—everyone is inside eating. You can tell it's noon because the shadow is directly under the car, which only happens at noon when the sun is straight overhead.

The car must belong to the people who live in the house behind it. It seems from the condition of the house that they care more about their house than their car.

I like how everything is placed in this picture—the car centered, with the line between the car doors going up to the line between the houses. And I like how the leaves on the tree are bunched up. They look beautiful the way they stretch over the roofs.

Looking at this car in the hot sun, battered and alone, makes me feel a sense of loneliness. But after lunch when the kids come outside, everything will be different. Since I live on a block where all the houses are connected, I would like a chance to play tag games or hide-and-seek with them in the driveways between the houses.

## BACKYARD ADVENTURE

The boys in this picture look like they are tightrope walking on clotheslines crisscrossing the backyards. But they are not. If you look closely, you can see that they are about to jump into a pool. It's a hot summer day and the roses are blooming. The boys are standing with their backs to the row of cozy houses that look like toys stacked side by side. They are having an adventure close to home.

## INSIDE OUT

There are a lot of things in this picture—backyards, clotheslines, fire escapes, electrical wires, wooden fences, and a furry dog leaning on a windowsill looking down at everything. I think it's kind of funny because that's the sort of thing people do. I wonder exactly what the dog is looking at. It could be looking at a bird or a cat, a squirrel climbing a tree or scurrying on the wires. It's hard to tell.

This picture of a dog stuck inside looking out at the world that it would like to be in reminds me of times when I can't go out, and I have to imagine myself where I want to be.

## NEW BABY, NEW FEELINGS

The boy in this picture could be thinking many thoughts. One might be, "I'm not getting enough attention" or "I wish you would just go away." He is standing where his mom can't see him, and the look on his face is a mix of loneliness, sadness, and curiosity. He is probably thinking that he wants to be little again so his mother can look at him the same way she is looking at his baby sister. It is the middle of the afternoon in the summertime. It must be hot outside because they aren't wearing very much, and also because you wouldn't take a baby out of the house, especially a newborn dressed like that, in the winter or fall.

I like how this picture was taken. How the mom is gently holding the baby, how the son is watching her longingly, the time of year, the time of day, *everything*.

## WORK'S REWARDS

I like the way this picture looks. There are boxes thrown all around the ground, the cellar doors are open, and it looks like a lot of things are going on. And above all that there is a boy working in the window. He looks like he's concentrating. His head is down and his body is twisted, he's kind of kneeling, and his arms look like he's swinging a baseball bat. He could be working to help his family pay bills — or to earn money to buy something he really wants.

A while ago I collected cans to make money. I called it "dumpster diving." I went around my neighborhood with a shopping cart, looking in people's trash for bottles and cans to deposit. I started small, making about five dollars every time I went out. Then when I became more experienced, I made twice as much. At first it seemed fun to look forward to having a lot of money. But then as I did it more and more, the work itself became more rewarding. I still have some of it saved in my money box. In the end, work pays off in many ways. When you work — do something hard, you can look back on what you did and say, "I did it."

## A PLACE OF THEIR OWN

I love tree houses—most kids do. Tree houses are places where you can be alone by yourself. They are places where you can do a lot of things. The top of my list would be looking at baseball cards and reading about baseball.

The tree in the middle of the picture has pieces of wood nailed across it for steps. They look like kids made them from scraps of wood that they found. The steps must be going to a tree house.

The house right by the tree house is abandoned. I wonder what kind of family lived there. I'll never know for sure, but I know they wanted their children to have a place of their own. They must have cared about their feelings, their happiness.

## BABYSITTING BLUES

It is a fall day. It's probably windy because the leaves are scattering around as if they are trying to find a specific place on the ground to stay. I like that the fences make all different types of patterns, and the cobblestones are in an up-and-down design.

The boy in this picture is strolling a baby up the street. In my opinion he has a lot of stress in his life. The baby must be his brother or sister, and seems like it's squirming—maybe it wants a bottle or it misses its mom. It sort of looks like it's tired of being outside. The boy probably feels like he wants to stop babysitting so he can play with kids his own age. Both the boy and the baby look like they are sick of this stroll.

I know the feeling—to want to get something over with. The door to the car behind him is open. Maybe someone just drove up in the car, and they are carrying groceries into the house, and he will not have to babysit much longer.

## A LONG WAIT REWARDED

The long shadows show that it is evening. The dog must have been waiting for a long time for his owner to come home. That's why he is so excited and he is jumping up to greet him. You can see how his tail is blurred from wagging. I like the shadow of the dog against the house, and the shadows of the shapes and lines of the fence on the dog—making an odd alphabet, like a baby would make.

I know how it feels to wait—when I was little I used to wait for my mom to come home from work. My dad and I used to sing a song that we made up called "Mommy Come Home" to make me feel better. The dog being so excited reminds me of how I used to feel after my long wait.

# LONE PIGEON

I think it's interesting that there are two kinds of houses in this picture. There's a pigeon house and a people house. To me one of the houses looks like a barn. In fact, pigeons are city birds, and this picture was taken in Brooklyn.

The lone pigeon looks beautiful standing on a little shelf in the sunlight. Although, I think it's kind of odd that you can only see one bird in the coop, because pigeons live in flocks and you usually see them together. It must be that the other birds are out flying. Pigeons fly around their coop in circles because they want to keep it in sight. Maybe this pigeon doesn't want to be flying with the others — maybe he just wants to be alone.

In a way, this pigeon staying close to home reminds me of my dog Stringy. If we let him out of the house he would just wait by the door. But if we let my other dog, his sister Lia, out she would explore the outside world a little bit and then come back — like the pigeons that are out flying. Pigeons that live in coops and my dogs are alike in a way. It doesn't matter if they roam around or stay close — in the end you would get the same conclusion . . . coming back home.

## TREE DREAMING

The boy in this picture is standing in a tree looking out and day-dreaming. It looks to me like his friends are walking away and he is left alone all by himself. It could be because they wanted to do something he didn't want to do, like play video games, so he climbed up the tree to think. Maybe he wants to feel the wind or the sun, or maybe he just wants to stay away from home.

Sometimes I want to get away from home and see all the things you can see in the world, and in a tree you have a better view. I like the way the telephone poles that you can see beneath the arching branch go way down the street till you can't see them anymore. This picture reminds me of how my mind wanders sometimes.

## EMPTY, IMAGINING FULL

This picture is about a boy looking into a vacant lot and imagining. He might be thinking about who used to live there, or the shape the shadow makes, or what kind of games he and his friends would like to play there. My friends and I would probably play catch and throw the ball against the wall — play running bases, maybe tag and street games like Red Devil. I think it's beautiful to turn something empty into something full.

## THE TOUGH SPOT

Whenever a father does something around his 3, 4, or 5 year old, the child will usually copy him. When I was little that's what I did. I think the dad is a fireman because he has a mug with #1 FIREM___ on it (you can't see the 'AN' on the side). There are bills on the counter and he's looking through the classifieds. Maybe he can't pay all of the bills and he's looking for another job. There's a piece of the classifieds torn off on the counter — it could be a job that he might want. The drapes behind them make a beautiful triangle shape above their heads, and there is a wedding picture hung next to them on the wall that shows a happier time in the dad's life.

This picture showing a father with a young child resting their heads on their arms, at home, with bills, possibly looking for a new job, makes me want to cry. But I hold the tears back. It makes me thankful for what I have.

## LONELY DRIVEWAY

I like how the sheet looks lonely blowing in the wind. It makes a sad shadow on the concrete. The garage looks like it has room for one more car. Maybe the people who live there have another car that they are using. They could have just driven out and that is why the gate is open. The driveway looks old, like it has been driven on a lot—it's cracked and broken. If cars had feelings, I think the car in the garage would be lonely. Looking at this picture reminds me of being left behind.

# FENCE FLYING

The kid climbing reminds me of me climbing on spiky fences. He makes an odd shape — twisted, balancing on the fence, trying not to fall. If the picture were taken a few seconds later, he would look completely different. Climbing is something he might like to do alone when his parents or babysitter are not looking because he probably is not allowed to do it. His friends aren't around to play with him, so he plays by himself. He might live in one of the apartment buildings in the background, and his mother doesn't let him go too far from home. His playground is the vacant lot behind the fence. Maybe he wants to fly, because when I climb I sort of feel like I'm flying. When I climb I also feel a sense of danger because if I fall I could get very hurt. I like to climb fences because climbing is as close to flying as I'm going to get.

## LAUNDRY LIGHTNING

A mother has hung her family's laundry up. It shouldn't take long to dry. It is a cloudless day and there is a slight breeze. The cracks on the side of the building are there because people have pulled on the clothesline for years. I think they look like lightning. To think about lightning when you're looking at a picture of cracks on the side of a building on an ordinary sunny day is a magical thing.

## PIGEON COOP BOY

Looking at birds usually makes me feel calm. Birds can't hurt you and they are graceful. I think that's how the boy feels because he looks comfortable—his arms and legs are relaxed and his eyes are closed. The pigeons must be happy to get out after being inside for a while, but they are loyal to the boy because they are not flying away. They are staying all around him. I think the boy is good to the pigeons—he feeds them, brings them water, and opens the door knowing they won't leave him. It's great to know you can trust someone or something.

One day, when I was about 3, I found a bird in my backyard with a broken wing. I fed him and bandaged his wing and cared for him. It was a rainy day when I found him, and he looked so sad that I named him "Sad Bird." I think I felt the same way about Sad Bird that the boy does towards his pigeons. I trusted Sad Bird not to fly away too far from our house and to always come back. I knew he needed love and care, and caring for him felt good because I knew I was helping him.

I'd like to think that Sad Bird comes back sometimes and feeds on the crumbs that I leave behind when I eat bread in the backyard. I'd love to care for him again.

## WELCOMING SPRING

When I'm in a rush, I'm sometimes careless with my things and I throw them around. It seems to me as if the kids who own these bikes were in a hurry to get inside, probably because it's suppertime from the look of the long shadows. It looks like it's spring. There are no leaves on the trees or on the ground. It's warm enough to ride bikes, but the swimming pool is still covered. Spring is when kids get to play outside after being cooped up all winter. The tree in the yard is reaching over to the neighbor's tree, touching it and making an arch, kind of welcoming spring in and all the things to look forward to.

# AN IMPORTANT LESSON

This picture is a bird's eye view of two dogs and three backyards. I wonder why the dogs are out there without someone or something to play with? Usually an owner would have a reason for doing that. Maybe they are guard dogs or they are out there to get some exercise. It reminds me of when I had two dogs. When no one was home — when I was at school or playing little league — I liked knowing that they had each other. It's the same for dogs and people, they both need a companion . . . a friend.

It looks like there is construction being done in the backyard on the left. Construction reminds me of moving because the purpose of it is to make something new, or to make a change. Moving is a change. I try not to think about it because I'm not crazy about change and I don't want to move. I'm lucky to have not experienced moving (I have lived in the same house my whole life).

But the thing is, I've experienced someone dying which was a major change. That someone was one of my dogs. Actually, my dog dying was an important experience for me. I cried, but I was also happy because I got to say the last words to her and the fact that I was there when she died was special to me. (The last words she heard are too important to me so I will not reveal them). At the time I had never seen anyone die. It was a very important life lesson. As for the other dog . . . he still needs a friend.

## GAME OVER, LAST ONE HOME

The dirt field is sloppy and muddy compared to the neat houses across the street. Kids have the freedom to be messy when they play outside. They are not expected to act the way they have to at home. There is only one boy in the picture, but there are too many footprints for him to have made them by himself. It looks like the game might be over and he is alone — the last one to go home. He is on the ground clutching the football, caked up with mud. It looks like he played hard, I wonder if his team won or lost? It would be a shame if he lost after trying so hard. I think it's kind of fun to get dirty — giving it your all — diving and sliding when you play sports. But when your team loses you sometimes feel bad . . . disappointed. When you lose it makes you feel empty, like you didn't do anything when you really did.

## ABOUT TIME

The boy is leaning on his jacket that he put over the fire hydrant. It must be late in the afternoon. The day started out cold and ended up warm, so he took his jacket off. It feels like spring. The paw prints in the sidewalk were made when the cement was wet a long time ago. Both the boy and the dog are waiting. Something is yet to happen, but nothing is happening in the moment. This picture is about time.

## JIGSAW SYMMETRY

This picture reminds me of a jigsaw puzzle. It could be accidental, but I'm sure it is meant to be that way because it's so symmetrical and because the things in the picture fit together perfectly. I see symmetry in things that I love, like baseball and chess and in numbers. When I find symmetry in the world, it gives me something to think about. For instance, I saw an ad for "Drivers Wanted" on a car with a phone number that looked special—it was 222-2222, and that number kept popping into my head all day.

For me, symmetry is order. When my room is messy I usually feel like something isn't complete, because I don't have space to work or play. It's the same thing with thinking. When your brain is cluttered you can't think straight. In this picture everything seems to be in the right place—the two walls, the lot, the row of houses in the background, the sky, even the shadows. If I could, I would live in a world that was as in order as this picture. Symmetry is beauty.

## SLEEPING TEENAGER, SHADOW DRAGON

I wonder what the teenager was thinking before he went to sleep on the park bench. It looks like it's a hot day, and he'd be better off under a shady tree. His body makes a zigzag shape with his arms crossed and his hands drooped down like dog ears. The sun is directly overhead and the boy is making a shadow that reminds me of a chess opening that's called "The Dragon." He wrapped his head up and covered it. Maybe he doesn't want us to see his face or he is blocking the sun from his eyes. I think it looks like he wants to escape from his life. This picture makes me feel sad. In my life I try to confront my problems — the things I need to work on.

## SNEAKER TREE

This is an ordinary block with ordinary houses and ordinary cars and ordinary trees. But the special thing about this block is the tree with around forty sneakers hanging from it. Anyone who happens to be walking or driving by must wonder how the sneakers got up there.

I imagine it happened on a summer night when kids were playing some variation of tag or hide-and-seek in the street. Then one kid, the wildest kid in the group, stood in the middle of the street, tied the laces together, and threw his sneakers in the tree to get attention. After that everyone copied him.

Kids copy other kids when they think something is daring or exciting. (I've done that kind of thing before, and it didn't pay off.) Because it was summer and the tree was full of leaves, nobody noticed. Now it's winter and there are no leaves on the tree and the shoes can be seen by everyone. This sneaker tree is more than a reminder of fun, it's a monument to what those kids did that summer night.

## ROOFTOP FREEDOM

The boy in this picture is up on a roof spreading his arms out probably to feel the wind. I'll bet he's a sports fan because he is wearing the jersey of a basketball player and a hat with a "G" on it. It stands for the Grays, an old Negro League baseball team.

I think he's on the roof because he wants to be away from home and feel free. It looks like a scene from a movie. A scene where the boy just did something good and he wants to feel the wind brush up against his body. It must feel like flying being up there with nobody around to see you.

I sometimes like to be alone and sing a little tune to myself or act something out, something that I do by myself because if I did it in front of people I'd feel embarrassed. This picture reminds me of me because what I'm trying to say is that feeling like you're flying, being alone, and feeling free are all gifts of life.

## JUNKYARD DOG

This dog isn't a household pet—he is a junkyard dog and he is surrounded by junk. I like how a lot of things in the picture lead to the dog. A diagonal beam lying on the ground, a ladder and a pole, even the grooves in the sidewalk seem like they form lines that point to him.

The dog is drinking out of a coffee cup. I wonder if the man in the back left it there for him, or if someone else left it there not knowing the dog would drink from it. (My dog Stringy would never drink or eat anything that anyone left out, but his sister Lia would steal food when we weren't looking.)

It must be rough being a junkyard dog, having to stay there for a long time watching for junk thieves on the dirty street. I wonder if that's why they have a reputation for being mean. I think it is. My family gives my dog a lot of love and care. It doesn't look like this dog gets much of either. I hope someday he will.

## A REALIZATION OF LOVE

The shadow in this picture is a father looking down at his baby with his hands in his pockets wondering how to love and take care of his newborn. They are in a garden. The father is standing in the sun, but he put his baby on a furry blanket under a plant in the shade. Fathers should always make little sacrifices for their babies and their children. Now that I'm older I've realized a lot of things about the differences between mothers and fathers, but they have one thing in common — love.

## A DIFFICULT QUESTION

This picture is about two girls, a woman, and a question. They are in the backyard and it looks like the two girls have just asked their mother something. The girl on the right is shy, she is biting her nails and keeping a distance. The girl in the middle is older and bolder — tougher and more willing to ask. She has gone right up to her mother, and her younger sister is counting on her. She is looking straight at us waiting for an answer.

They could've asked, "Can we go out to play?" or "Can we use your make-up to play dress up?" or "Where is dad and when is he coming home?" The mother is looking away thoughtfully. Maybe the question is hard to answer. This picture makes me think of parents and children and what's difficult between them.

## WORKING TREE

This picture reminds me of the Robert Frost poem "Birches," because of how the tree is bent. The tree looks sad and beautiful with its thin branches hanging down. When I first saw it I thought the branches looked like long weeping blades of grass. In the poem there is a boy who likes to swing from birch trees. He plays games by himself that he makes up when he doesn't have work to do. There is a pulley and chain on the tree that my dad told me men use to lift engines out of cars so they can be worked on in the street. I wonder if kids play in the tree and climb up the limbs and swing down on the branches or slide down the chain. It all makes me think of poetry.

## PASSING DOWN LOVE

I wonder if the father in this picture is hoping that his baby will be interested in baseball when he gets older. My dad and I sometimes listen to baseball games on the radio together, and I'll bet there's a game on the radio next to the father's head. He is cuddling his baby on his chest and resting his head on his baseball glove. It is broken in and worn as if it has a history to it.

My glove has had a life to it, too — it shows its age. When I look at it, I remember all the great times and games I had with it. The father might think that his baby will someday enjoy his old mitt the same way he did when he played with it. I can imagine someday giving my old baseball gloves to my kids and letting them use them. The things that I'll pass down to my children and do with them are the things that were a big part of my life and were closest to me.

## FIND THE DOG

When I first looked at this picture, I asked myself, why was it taken? Then I looked harder and I realized why. There is a dog poking his head through the fence. I didn't see him at first because the dog looked like part of the vine. His muzzle and his ears look like leaves. It's lovely and funny at the same time. This picture reminds me that things aren't always what they appear to be when you first see them. And if you take your time and focus, you can discover the beauty in things.

## THE LOST UMBRELLA

There is a broken umbrella on the ground that the wind blew out of its owner's hands. But there are no puddles in the street and it's a sunny day, so this picture must have been taken a day or two after the rain. It looks like a father and son are crossing the street paying no attention to the parked car with a shattered windshield. There are bits of broken glass beside it and some dead leaves cluttering the street. The tilted umbrella creates a polygon-shaped shadow that looks as if it can fill in the empty part of the sky that the trees make. (You can see it better if you squint.)

This picture makes me feel the way I do when I lose something. Even if it's only a 50-cent ball, I really want it back. I think something that's mine is mine forever no matter what happens to it, and that I'm responsible to take care of it. I'll bet the person who lost this umbrella doesn't know that he helped make this wonderful picture.

## A DAY TO REMEMBER

I like how this picture is made—it has three parts. The interesting thing about it is that on the left side of the picture you can see the right side of the room because there is a mirror there. That's why the light is the same on both sides of the picture—it's the sun shining through the windows. In the middle, there is a fancy white candle, like a candle you might see at a wedding, and lined up with it is the darkened hallway that leads to the doors that go outside. It's daytime and most kids (including me) would rather be outside playing. I've noticed that older people don't usually move around that much and they stay in and watch TV a lot instead of going out. The man in the mirror is looking at the TV and the woman is looking away—maybe her mind is wandering, maybe she's remembering something from when they were young.

## A FAMILY PHOTO

It looks like the baby is going to have a bath because he has his shirt pulled over his head and his mother is holding a towel. The mother was undressing him when she looked in the mirror and saw how funny the shirt looked on his head. She stops and talks baby talk in a high-pitched tone, laughing, "oh, look how cute you are" or "how silly you look." The father sees what's going on and decides to take a family picture in the mirror. You know this picture was taken in a mirror because his wedding ring is on his right hand and it should be on his left hand. In a mirror things are reversed. The baby is looking at everything going on and hanging onto his mom's necklace. I like that the mom is making time to play with the baby and the father is not only taking the picture but he wanted himself in it. This looks like a family that enjoys being together. I'm glad because . . . this baby is me.